Things That Make U Go Hmmm . . .

Book #2 Marriage From A Single Perspective

Dr. Rhonda L. Gibbs

Things That Make U Go Hmmm . . .
Book #2 Marriage
From A Single Perspective
Copyright © 2006 by Dr. Rhonda L. Gibbs
All rights reserved

Printing by Falcon Books
San Ramon, California

Except for brief reviews, no part of this book may be reproduced by any means, without the written permission of the author.

adnohr press
drrlgibbs@aol.com

ISBN 10: 0-9754613-1-1
ISBN 13: 978-0-9754613-1-0

PRINTED IN THE UNITED STATES OF AMERICA

ACKNOWLEDGMENTS

Thanks . . .

To my family for their support of writing these series of books. Your collective strength helps to encourage me.

To my friends that believe in me. Your constant care and constructive criticism motivates me to think big.

To my editors who make this challenge possible. I am forever grateful for all of your time and efforts.

To my unfailing God, who gives me the wisdom and the humility to write about marriage.

Things That Make U Go Hmmm . . . Book #2
Marriage From A Single Perspective

Chapter 1

Observations

Many people say that experience is the best teacher. I would have to disagree with this statement in the case of marriage. I have never been married. However, I have observed many many marriages. At this time in my life, I feel that it is better not to learn from being married, but to learn from people who have been married.

One day I drove from Tulsa, Oklahoma to Dallas, Texas. As I was visiting a friend, he happened to have two other male friends at his home. Both of his friends were divorced. I begin to be my normal inquisitive self. I basically asked one question to these two strangers, "Did you both know the relationship that your wives had with their father before you married her?" The one guy said, "No." The other guy said, "I knew the relationship she had with her dad and it was not good." Bingo! One of the first rules of thumb in dealing with someone of the opposite is find out what kind of relationship they had with their parents. If it is a male, then find out what kind of relationship he has with his mother. If it is a female, then find out what kind of relationship that she has had with her father.

So many people that get involved with a male/female relationship never even deal with this issue. This is so basic and "fundamental" in developing a good male/female relationship. For example, if the male hates his mother, even to the point that he would hit her, most likely he will hit you after you say "I do". Why? How a man treats his mother is often times an indication of how he will treat his wife. Yes, there are some exceptions to the rule. However, it is worth exploring this issue before you say I do.

If a female has a bad relationship with her father then it will affect your marriage. Let's say that her father verbally abused her all her life. In many cases, the first time that the husband raises his voice in the marriage, memories of her childhood could come racing back to her mind. Do you think that she wants to make love after she has relived a part of her past she would prefer to forget? I don't think so!

Another great question that should be asked in a male/female relationship is, "How do you handle your anger?" Many times while couples are dating they are constantly on their best behavior. Therefore, you do not get to see your significant other in various levels of emotions. If you have never gotten angry before in your life, then you will get angry while you are married. Why? Because marriage is work! Sometimes you feel like working and sometimes you don't. The times that you do not feel like working will cause you to feel fits of rage or anger. Now, if you would have known that your spouse handles his or her angry by slamming the door, shutting down, or by venting to someone of the opposite sex, would you not have rethought getting some help in this area? Now, that you know how they handle their anger it is your choice to come to some agreement over your differences. If you cannot come to some nice resolution then the relationship will end. Are you sure that you want to be another divorce statistic?

One of the best ways to see if a person really has a bad temper is to put them in some type of competition. For instance, if he or she has a favorite way of working out like, playing basketball, softball, or tennis, watch them compete in their sport. As I play basketball full court every week, I see bad tempers and hear so much bad language. Hearing a four letter word comes out of someone's mouth happens after every turnover. It is amazing how easy it is for them to scream out in this way. These men usually display their anger by kicking the ball; throwing the ball a great distance, and sometimes just ready to swing at one of the players. Even though I am not there to get a date per se, I am so turned off by their lack of temperance. I would not consider anyone who carries himself this way in a gym. It is not like we are playing for money or that we even get some type of award for winning a nine point game. If a person can go off the handle in throwing the ball away one time, then just imagine what could happen if you made one major mistake in your dating relationship? It is important to learn how to disagree agreeably about mistakes that are made.

Chapter 2

Red flags

I often fly and talk with people on airplanes. On one trip I ask several married people this question. "While you were dating your spouse did you happen to see a red flag in the dating process? All of them said, "Yes." I would venture to say that when they saw the red flag, they chose to ignore it, think it was going to change, or were naïve about the red flag. In any case, now most of them have found themselves separated or divorce based on that red flag.

A red flag represents a warning. It is preparing you to be aware of something that may take place in the future. Often times we choose to ignore the red flags. We may even hear the siren going off and see the flashing light, but many times we ignore all the signals saying, "warning and be cautious". This is dangerous in any relationship. For example, if a woman was sexual abused by her uncle, and while you were dating her she would have a hard time in letting you get close to her, this is a definite red flag. If a woman dates a man who is thirty something, who lives at home with his mother, and cannot keep a job, this too is a red flag. Why do woman choose to ignore red flags like this? Then they wonder why they are behind in their bills. Maybe because your thirty something husband keeps forgetting to go to work everyday.

Why do we think that people are going to change once we marry them? In some cases they do change. In other cases, the person made up their mind about something and nothing will move them from their point of view. We must not believe the myth that people will change once they get married too so and so. For example, if a woman says that she does not want to have children, yes she could change her mind, but do not assume that she will. The desire to have children is usually a well thought out process for a lot of women. Now that you are married and she still has not changed her mind in this area, just support her decision.

Another red flag that I have seen in relationships is a person constantly giving you mixed messages. The person that I am spending quality time with will say one thing, but do something total different. Listen to me: "Action speaks louder than words." If he says that he loves you and never calls, watch out! If she says that she wants to spend more quality time with you, but never seems to make time for you, beware! People that send mixed messages are having a battle within themselves. One side of them is extremely excited about the relationship and the other side is afraid. Unless you have experienced a gripping fear in your own empirical experiences then you cannot appreciate that struggle of fear within the other person. For example, if a person is being physically abuse, almost everyone thinks why doesn't that person just get out of the relationship. Well, could it be that the fear of getting hit again is less than the fear of not having any place to go? The fear within that person is gripping when she / he stays and when she / he is trying to leave the relationship. They feel like they cannot win. Whichever fear is the greatest wins out.

So, if you are in a relationship and the man is giving you a mixed message, the part within him that is closer to his intimate feelings usually wins out. In other words, a man's loyalty to a woman is as deep as their least intimate message. That is why so many women get hurt. It looks like all is going well in the relationship, then all of a sudden you hear less and less from him. Then you do not hear from him again. What happen? What happened is that the fear within overtook the relationship. He could not deal with his own insecurities so he chose the easy way out. Believe me, if he was that weak then you are far better without him. Just be glad that you found out about his struggles before you said, "I do."

I was sitting on airplane next to a gentleman. I began telling him about this book. He and his wife do marriage-counseling training to couples from state to state. He was fascinated by my title and my insight to marriage. He later began to give his insight of a red flag that I have never pondered before. Check this out!

Imagine that a couple is dating for several months and the woman is really ready to get married. A matter of fact, she brings up getting married first. Consider the following set of questions:

Question 1: "Honey, how many friends can you say that you have had for fifteen years?"
Question 2: "How many friends have you had for ten years?"
Question 3: "How many friends have you had for 5 years?"

If all the answers are "None", pay attention to the sirens and red flags with such answers!

The person answers, "None." How many friends have you had for ten years? The person answers again, "None." Well, how many friends have you had five years? The answer is still, "None." Can you hear the sirens? Do you see any flashing lights? Are you sensing a signal that says precede with caution in your heart?

Listen, this person wants to spend the next 20, 30, or 40 years of his/her life with you and they cannot even tell you that they have had a friendship with anybody for five years. The flag cannot get any redder than that! You mean to tell me that you are going to put a ring on his/her finger and he/she does not even have one friend on this planet?

What does this say about this person? What kind of personality does he/she have that he/she has not developed one long lasting friendship. Based on your partner's past, how likely will he/she have a long lasting friendship with you? I call this person a "leech". "Leeches" are going to suck all of the life out of you because he/she wants you to meet their every need. I mentioned before that marriage is work, but you have not seen work until you are married to a leech.

It makes so much sense to check out a person's past friendship before you get so heavily involved with him / her. A person who has no friends is a dangerous person to be married to. If you choose to marry a person with this type of loner personality then you might as well plan to seek some outside help to keep a healthy relationship. The antithesis of this is a person with a lot of friends should be able to let you know what are the positive and negative comments that they are all saying about that person.

For those of you who married Mr. / Mrs. Leech, you need to finds ways for them to spend their time. For example, intentionally find ways that they can spend without you discussing the fact that if you want to make this relationship work, then you must quit clinging on to me so tight. Let them know that they could squeeze the very life out of you. So in order for our relationship to get healthy, then please give me some breathing room. Design a schedule together that encourages your spouse to return to those interests that made him / her who you fell in love with in the first place.

So what happens when I married "Mr. Insecure" and now he is walking out on me? Let him go and I must get some help. I can find help in pouring out my feelings toward a good friend, or finding a good psychologist. A good psychologist is one that is willing to take the time to listen to my pain, and is not so quick to give me answers.

Sex is such a major part of marriage. If a person has been sexually abuse before they have gotten married this must be discussed. Instead of the sexually experience is being enjoyable, it will often times feel disgusting because of the abuse in the past. Much professional counseling should be given in this area.

If the couple is already married and they are having problems in their sex life, I still encourage the couple to get some type of help in helping them overcome in their time of intimacy. Whether it is reading a good book, talking to a recovering person in this area, or group therapy, help is there for the asking.

It is very important to find ways to redirect your stressful situation. I usually find the best way for me to relieve stress is working out. A good full court basketball game does wonders for my tension. Also, I find playing with children or taking a long distance drive really relaxes me. If the person you are dating or are married to will not take care of you, then it is essential that you take care of yourself. If you will not take care of yourself then most likely not anyone else will either.

Finally, remember if you see a red flag while dating, it does not mean that you cannot marry that person. Just be glad that you saw it and now deal with it before you say, "I do." Pay now or pay later.

Chapter 3

Show Me The Money

Many people get a divorce because of a lack of money. Having financial troubles on top of other things going wrong in a marriage only makes life worst. There are a couple of things a single person can do before saying I do.

As you spend quality time with your significant other, finances usually come up in a conversation. For example, you could be talking about the monthly hassle of paying bills, buying gifts for a family member, or just balancing your checkbook. All of these subjects evolve around spending money. As one talks about spending money then the subject of debt could come up. As you talk about getting out of debt then you could say, "I want to get out of debt to help build my line credit." As the relationship develops, it would be very beneficial to get a copy of each other's credit report and discuss them in detail. By doing this, it can help you decided whether or not this is the person that you want to spend the rest of your life with.

You may ask, "What can a credit report tell you about a person?" A credit report can help you see what areas are priorities in one's spending. For example, if a person always pays their bills late, has two cars repossess and has filed bankruptcy three times, then maybe you might want to rethink saying "I do" to this person. Granted, this is an extreme case, but this is not an impossible situation.

A credit report can show how much financial integrity a person has. Someone with a history of outstanding credit card debt should be challenged in the dating period. It is like knowing that the person that you are about to marry is a habitual gambler and you never asked him why he/she has this problem. Later, after you are married for a couple of years, you wonder why you are struggling financially. You are barely paying the monthly bills, your paycheck is spent before your get it, and you never have any money in your saving account. Things that make U go hmmm . . . You knew he/she had problem gambling, and you also knew that he/she had outstanding credit cards history. However, you still chose to marry this person. Please check out the person's credit before you marry them. Do not gamble on whether or not the marriage will work out financially.

Not only is it important to check out a person's credit, but also do some investigation on a person's work history. Imagine dating someone who has never really had a decent job. They have worked at places that were more hobby opportunities versus a career job. Pay attention to how your partner behaves in public with his/her money! For example, when you go out to eat, how quickly do they offer to pay for both meals. What kind of tips does he/she leave behind? How quickly does he/she pay the bill? With cash or credit? Do you know why they prefer to use that form of currency? Sometimes you often have to pay and they seem to enjoy that. Maybe you go out to eat and he/she forgets his/her wallet. Could it be that this person really does not intend to get a real job? Some people just go through the motions from one relationship to the next. They do whatever they can to get a free meal.

In checking the work history of a person, if it is a man who has not had a great track record, watch out! A man who is not willing to work is a dangerous man. Unless you are willing to give up shopping, pampering, and eating, then you may want to reconsider dating this man. Even if he is tall dark and husband, being broke and lazy is never attractive.

Many people will see that a person has a streak a laziness in his/her personality while they are dating. Evidence of laziness can be seen in how they take care of their car, house, themselves and their job. After a person gets laid off a good job sometimes it is hard to get off the sofa. Meanwhile, you know that you saw all the warning signs of being lazy while dating, but now you expected them to be a workaholic once they have said, "I do." Love is not that blind. If it is, then you will be in love but broke.

The other extreme of dealing with a person's work history is seeing whether or not the person is married to their work. I remember dating a dedicated musician. He was always in the studio practicing. He could hardly keep a good job because he was constantly developing his music skills. I knew if we got married, he would be more committed to his music than he would be to me. Music was his world! I knew that I did not want to be in second place in his heart.

Many people get so involved in their careers that their families always take back seats. I have seen this happen to athletes, movie stars, ministers, musicians, and almost any other profession that you can think of. I remember hearing about a man who was so into his church that his wife divorced him. The wife thought that he should not give up the church because of the divorce because that is what he was good at doing. Which career is more important than keeping your family together? Unfortunately, many people slowly but surely get more in love with their careers than their spouses. What a sad scenario to be in!

As single people spend quality time with their significant other, it is important to observe how much time that person spends on his/her job. Have you ever been on a date and your date spends more time talking on his/her cell phone than he/she spends with you? It is okay to take an occasionally call, but if your dates take calls from the office every time you go out then you might want to see who / what your partner is planning to be really married to.

There are several things that you can look for if a person is married to his/her job. You may want to answer these questions first:

- How much time does he or she spends at work?
- How much time does he or she spends at work when he or she is not at work?
- Does this person take business calls while he/she are on vacation?
- Does this person talk about his/her job more that anything other topic?

- Is his/her cell phone connected to their ear?

If you have found yourself married to a person who is always looking for a hand out, then plan on having a frustrated marriage. You will find that the relationship is not a 50-50 deal. Try more like a partnership of 80-20. This will eventually wear you out. It becomes draining always giving more into the marriage then the other person is willing to give. If you want to see changes, it is important to be extremely verbal in the areas that drive you crazy. For example, if you are constantly finding yourself taking the initiative in doing special activities then let them know how you feel about this. Encourage them to take the initiative in the next family event and let them make all of the detailed plans. If that person is not very organized, you may want to briefly check their contacts to reassure that the event will happen successfully.

These are just a few things to examine to see if a person is married to his/her job. <u>Remember</u>; if you are a person that marries someone with these kinds of qualities then expect to have some difficulties in your marriage. You may have a lot of money but you may not have much quality time with your spouse.

Chapter 4

Can't Keep It A Secret

Do you remember, in your childhood, when you were on the playground and one of your buddies said, "I have a secret. I have a secret." Then he/she would say, "If I tell you then you cannot tell anyone else." Of course you always agreed just so you could hear the secret. After they told you the secret, you got so excited you wanted to tell the world. You felt like a kid with a new toy. Being in love often feels that way. You meet this person of the opposite sex and you just want to tell the world about this new toy in your life. What happens when that "new toy" hurts you? What happens when that "new toy" breaks your heart?

I have walked a many persons through the pain of a broken heart. This is one of the hardest things to deal with. Usually the spouse has committed some type of infidelity and the other spouse is ready to walk out of the relationship. The struggle is that the spouse who did not commit infidelity is still in love with their spouse. The pain is heart breaking. The best thing that I could do for them is just listening and be empathetic. Many of these relationships ended in divorce, but some are still holding on to their marriage.

Many people ask me how can you be over thirty and never be married? My response silences them. I tell them that I am very happy in being single. I do not experience loneliness. I maybe have an occasional lonely moment but not a lonely lifestyle. I let them know I desire to get married, "but I refuse to be married and lonely." After that statement, the silence begins. I have met too many married and lonely people in my life time. I choose not to be one of them.

When a single person experiences a broken heart several things can happen. They can gain weight, loose weight, spend money, workout more, jump into a rebounding relationship, or never want to be in a relationship again. Depending on the personality of the person who got hurt at least one of these things will occur.

I recently told one of my friends that if this were to ever happen to me then I would go into the next relationship with much caution. I also said that I would not tell anybody that I was in the new relationship so that I would not have to let everyone know that I got hurt. She said, "You can't keep being in love a secret. It would be all over your face." I knew she was telling the truth. Being in love is so exciting, and I would not be able keep it a secret.

Many people have told me that they cannot define love. Well, I beg to differ. I have experienced love as a feeling that occurs deep down in your bellow every time you just think of that person. Love is not deaf, dumb, or blind. Love is something that a person should grow in and not just fall into. When you grow into love, it is most likely to last. If you fall in love or, as I prefer to see it, stumble into love then it will most likely may not last.

As I was teaching in college, one student ask me, "Dr. Gibbs why do you think that so many people get a divorce?" I said, "Because I feel that most people fall in lust instead of growing in love." I am glad to say that not one person in the classroom disagreed with me.

Love is willing to take its time whereas lust is always, in a hurry. Lust never wants to wait. Lust is deaf, dumb, and blind. In a lot of cases when people have rushed into a physically relationship it did not have anything to do with love but all to do with lust. Once that feeling of lust wears off then what happens to the relationship?

How much longer could the relationship last if both parties do not stumble into a blind relationship but gradually grow in their love for one another? What would happen if the relationship were built on genuine friendship rather than on one hot steamy moment? How many times does it take for us to realize that a one-night stand of lust can ruin so many things in our lives? Why choose lust when I can choose love that could last so much longer?

It is so important to be yourself in the relationship. If you have to hide feelings of joy in a new relationship, then that is not good. I often struggle with phony people. It is so important to be real. Even when I go on a job interview I think, a person cannot fake being real. With that mindset I go in with confidence to be questioned about that job opportunity. This is the same mindset I have in dealing with male-to-female relationships.

If I act fake then it won't last. If they act fake then I am not interested. So why not just be yourself because you cannot keep it a secret of whom you really are anyway. The sooner you come to deal with the real you in the relationship the more quality the relationship becomes. Don't waste time playing games. I often tell people the only games I play are basketball, tennis, and golf. Playing mind games only puts the true growth of the relationship on hold. Be real. Be genuine and don't keep who you are a secret. The unfolding of time will cause you to blossom into the real red rose of who you are really trying to be.

Now in dealing with marriage, I believe I have found the secret of keeping your spouse forever. Once you have been married for a long time you really get to know a person's strengths and weaknesses. You know what makes him / her happy and what makes them sad. You know his/her favorite food and what he/she likes to drink. You know your spouse intimately that you even know his/her insecurities.

Insecurities are those areas in our lives that make us feel uncomfortable at times. I believe that's the secret of keeping you spouse forever is to help your spouse identify those insecurities and to help him / her address them.

For example, a person should never make jokes about a woman's weight or a man going bald. These are too extremely sensitive areas for most people. If it were true that these are two illustrations of insecurities for many people, what would happen if a person began to build their spouse up in these areas? If one would encourage their spouses in their insecure areas of their lives, then it would make our spouses feel so good about them. For example, if your spouse is feeling insecure about his/her body then reassure him / her how beautiful he/she really looks. A compliment spoken from the heart can take a person a long way.

If you are a couple who are struggling in your marriage, try this little secret. Begin today finding ways to build your spouse up in the areas of their insecurities. Discovering the areas of insecurities is usually not the difficult part of this exercise, but consistently encourage them in their points of weaknesses in the harder task. Watch how your relationship begins to grow in communication, in compassion, and in intimacy. You may even experience some of those feelings of the positive dating emotions unexpectedly. Do not stop finding ways to build your spouse up and this could be the beginning of keeping them for life. I could no longer keep this a secret.

Just recently, I had a dear friend remind me that I told her this statement years ago. She went into her marriage practicing this basic secret.

She began building her husband up from the start of her marriage. Now she and her husband have been married for over ten years. Her words to me were, "Dr. Gibbs, it really works."

How does all of this apply to a single person? Because everyone has insecurities, this principle also works in a dating relationship. The more time you spend with a person, the better you get to know them. If the right questions are asked and the things are continually done, one can figure out quite easily what insecurities a person's has.

Once you have noticed what that person's insecurities are, then it is important to be aware of how your partner handles them. For example, if you and your significant other both play tennis and he is always competing with you in a negative way, by laughing at you every time you miss a easy shot, then this could be a possible red flag in your relationship. You will hear it in his conversations with his friends, your friends, and even when you are casually just talking about tennis one on one. Later it could get to the point that your love for the game of tennis decreases because the struggle of his insecurities no longer makes the game fun.

Another example of how a person handle's his/her insecurities in a dating relationship is not only being aware of the things that you have in common, but also of the things that you do different. If I love my job and he does not like his job then this could create problems. As I describe how lovely my day went at work it could make him feel sad about how much he dislikes his job. As conversations about our employment occur weekly, it could create feelings of insecurity within him. This also could start emotions of resentment toward me. Later our relationships gradually are affected in a negative way. I would not be surprise if the relationship ends because of the constant challenges that these insecurities stir within a person. If you want to have a healthy relationship then your insecurities can't be kept a secret.

Chapter 5

Being Whole

Is marriage really 50/50? Why do we say, "Meet my better half?" When we go to weddings and candles are being lit, should we blow out the two individual candles when we light the one big candle? What does it mean to be a whole person anyway? Have you ever met a person who was supposedly well adjusted and it did not seem like their mental elevator door was even open let alone the elevator door did not rise to the top? What happens when Mr. Lonely meets Ms. Lonely?

Many people say that they are whole, but struggle with doing the daily routines of life. For example, it may be hard for them to keep a job, or keep their homes clean, or just being able to have a decent conversation with someone on the street. People must first feel comfortable with themselves before they can interact with others. If a person does not like himself how is he going to enjoy a relationship with a nice man or woman?

Your wholeness should not be based on someone else. It is very important to know who you are before you get involved in a serious male/female relationship. You should know who you are apart from the person you are dating. You should know what makes you happy and what makes you sad. You should know what makes you angry and what makes you glad. Do you like to talk to people who intellectually stimulate you or are casual conversations just fine? How important are physical features to you? Does a college degree help you choose whether you would go out with a person or not? Is money an issue? These are just a few things to consider.

When I was working on my doctoral studies, I remember that my professor gave some

Chapter 5

Being Whole

Is marriage really 50/50? Why do we say, "Meet my better half?" When we go to weddings and candles are being lit, should we blow out the two individual candles when we light the one big candle? What does it mean to be a whole person anyway? Have you ever met a person who was supposedly well adjusted and it did not seem like their mental elevator door was even open let alone the elevator door did not rise to the top? What happens when Mr. Lonely meets Ms. Lonely?

Many people say that they are whole, but struggle with doing the daily routines of life. For example, it may be hard for them to keep a job, or keep their homes clean, or just being able to have a decent conversation with someone on the street. People must first feel comfortable with themselves before they can interact with others. If a person does not like himself how is he going to enjoy a relationship with a nice man or woman?

Your wholeness should not be based on someone else. It is very important to know who you are before you get involved in a serious male/female relationship. You should know who you are apart from the person you are dating. You should know what makes you happy and what makes you sad. You should know what makes you angry and what makes you glad. Do you like to talk to people who intellectually stimulate you or are casual conversations just fine? How important are physical features to you? Does a college degree help you choose whether you would go out with a person or not? Is money an issue? These are just a few things to consider.

When I was working on my doctoral studies, I remember that my professor gave some important steps in order to be a healthy single person. One of those points was to have friends of the opposite sex. Just being around them will help you feel better about yourself. It is great to ask them questions about the opposite gender so that you can get that other perspective. Many times I had questions about why the man would do certain things. I would just pick up the phone and call a close friend who could give me insight on the male perspective. This always made me feel better. Plus the companionship is also healthy. In putting this to test, I would have to agree that this has helped me develop into healthier single person.

Laugher is a good medicine in helping you develop being whole. There is so much stress in life that if you do not laugh then you will cry. I have had privileged to teach public speaking. I usually let my students choose one topic and they do three speeches. Speech one is the problem, speech two is the cause, and speech three is the solution. After they have given at least three practice speeches without getting graded, they are now prepared for their first graded speech.

Before the first person gets up to give his/her speech, I usually put on the video entitled, "Afros and Bellbottoms." Sinbad is a comedian who compares the youth of the 70's verses the youth of the 90's. In the last class I taught, many of the students were born in the 50's. I have never seen a class laugh so hard at this video! They could relate to every story that he told. The laughter grew louder and louder as the video played on.

You may ask, "Why would a college professor show a stand up comedian before giving their first series of speeches? The answer is simple: The more a person laughs, the more relaxed he/she tends to be. If a person relaxes before giving his/her oral presentations, then the speaker will be less nervous and stressful. Laughing helps a person relieve stress and can help develop wholeness. Anytime a person is under too much stress whether it be a job, a project, or in a relationship, watching a good comedian or having a good laugh can relieve some tension.

Another way of developing your wholeness is having accountability with close friends. Accountability does not seem to be a popular word in the 21st century. Most people just like to do their own thing. It like the attitude, "If it feels good, do it." However, sometimes other people can see things about you that you cannot see. I have intentionally had accountability partners since I was a teenager. I knew that I wanted to do great things in my life, to make a difference. So I wanted my inner circle of friends to be able to pull my coattail when I was going in the wrong direction. This inner circle was made up of friends who are at least ten years older than me. Once again, I was learning from their life experiences so that I would not make the same mistakes.

Even to this day, I stay accountable to people who can tell me what I need to hear as well as what I want to hear. It does not always feel good, but in the long run it saves me some headaches. It is important to develop accountability so that others can help you become whole. Recently, I called up several friends to ask them to meet with me a couple of times a year to challenge me. I want them to be able to ask me the tough questions. As they regularly meet with me, it will help me to continue to develop wholeness and become a stronger person of integrity. Being accountable to someone when you are a single person is really not that popular, as I mentioned before, however, why bump your head when you have watched your mentor bump theirs.

Chapter 6

Learning From Other People

It's just amazing to me how we can watch a person touch a hot stove and get burnt and then we follow up by touching the stove too. One would think that we would learn from someone else's mistakes. It is just like we know that scientists have not invented 100% birth control, but many are still wondering how, even when practicing "safe sex", they got pregnant or became infected with AIDS. How can a single person learn from a married person? It might be good by asking the right questions to the right person.

Asking questions is something that I have practiced for years. I believe that I have gotten far in life at a quick pace because I have asked the right questions. In the previous chapter, I'd mentioned that most of my friends are older than me. It is essential that singles ask couples, who seem to have a good marriage, about marriage. Just recently I was sitting in a restaurant talking to a lady who loves being married. She began to give me advice about things that happen behind closed doors. Here are some of what she thought would be important for single ladies to know before getting married.

Behind Closed Doors

"How could some one get married and not know so much?" That is exactly how I felt. There were so many things that no one told me. Marriage is **not 50/50.** Both husband and wife have to give 100% or you cannot survive. There are times when the husband will give 70% and the wife will give 30% and there will be times when the wife will give 70 and the husband will give 30%. But you both are giving as much as you can due to illness, family situations, financial issues, but you are in marriage together to give to each other, not to take from the other until there is no more to take.

When I was a stay-at-home mom, I did the majority of the cleaning, laundry, grocery shopping, and child-care so when my husband was home we could enjoy our family together. When I went to nursing school, my husband did the laundry, shopping, ran to the ball field, cleaned the house. Together we accomplished what had to be done without worrying whose job it was.

No one told me that sex begins in the morning when you get up, not at the end of a long day when you fall into bed. To have an awesome experience when you get in bed at the end of your day, you need to nurture that part of you marriage all day long. Being a nag and harping about jobs not done all day does not make your spouse feel like jumping in bed and making mad passionate love to you. Being a nag makes your spouse feel like avoiding the bedroom at all cost.

That good morning kiss, the hug as you hurry to get ready to go to work sets the pace for the day. Tell your husband you will be thinking of him today, you will be looking forward to seeing him in the evening. Let him see you put on sexy underwear and tell him it makes you think of him all day.

Call your wife and let her know you are thinking about her during the day. Talk about the two of you. Buy her sexy lingerie that is comfortable and compliments her body type. If you want to see your wife in something other than flannel, you may have to give up keeping the air conditioner on 60 degrees! If the thermostat is set on 60 and this is keeping you from wearing something other than sweats, tell your husband.

Write a hot little love note and leave it on the dash of his car or in his wallet. You don't have to spend a fortune on expensive lingerie. Watch for sales, sometimes the scantier the item the bigger the sale. Keep a few "5 minute" items on hand to surprise your husband. Ask him what he likes to see you in and try wearing it at least just once.

Get rid of the old t-shirts and ragged phi's when you get married. My husband used to get up at 3:00 A.M. to go to work. When he went to work he liked to watch me sleeping in something sexy. Satin p.j.'s, something soft and feminine go a long way to give your husband something to think about all day in a world full of women who are just waiting for your husband to start looking. You can be comfortable and sexy at the same time.

Keep your bedroom your own sanctuary for the two of you. Decorate it to be inviting and romantic. Don't use your room for an office/TV/bedroom. Keep the kids in their own rooms. It makes for a healthier, happier, rested family when everyone has their own bed.

I once overheard a young wife state "Our marriage is not based on sex; that doesn't have first priority in our house". Another young wife once stated "Sex is like under age drinking; it is no longer fun when it is legal. When we had sex before marriage it was more exciting." These statements come from women in their late twenty's to early thirty's. How sad that these women are so quick to throw out a vital part of their marriages. I also once heard a young man explain to a wife complaining of his sexual interest in her: "What is the point of getting married if it were not for the sex; I can do anything else with a friend" He has a point. A husband or wife who does not take care of the sexual part of his or her relationship or do not accept and enjoy this part of his or her marriage is inviting someone else to fill this need.

We are made to be sexual beings; to deny this is asking for trouble. As a young bride my husband worked a job that presented many opportunities for him to be invited out by attractive young women. I made sure my husband was well taken care at home. If my husband had to travel on business, I made sure the candles were lit, music was on, and he had a memorable send off. When he came home I greeted him at the door looking my best, and if the kids were gone he had a memorable homecoming.

Keep the doors of communication open to discussing your likes and dislikes when making love. Be sensitive to each other's needs. The more you are pleasing to your husband/wife, the more you will be pleased yourself. Be honest with each other. If you don't like something, don't fake it. You may spend the rest of your life pretending to like something that really turns you off. If you say you don't like something follow that statement with a suggestion of what you do like. Sex doesn't have to always happen at 10:00 P.M. with the lights turned off. A young co-ed I know was very concerned that her parents had no relationship at all because all she ever heard was her dad snoring all night long. I reminded her that her dad was a farmer, and came home for lunch everyday while she was at school.

No one told me that in order to have romance in my marriage it was just as much my responsibility as my husbands. I would wait for him to ask my out on a date, wait for him to plan a romantic evening. Finally it occurred to me that I could plan a date, I could plan a romantic evening, and if I waited on my husband it might not happen. You don't have to spend a fortune to have a romantic evening. Don't add financial stress to your marriage by always having to go to an expensive restaurant or hotel. Be creative, get rid of the kids, fix his or her favorite dinner, and plan an evening at home. When was the last time you "made out"? Remember when you used to flirt with your husband or wife? Don't stop! That look across the room that whispered comment as you pass by each other while you do the dishes will go a long way to keep the fire lit between you. When you are at a large gathering of friends, don't forget whom you came with. Use that special smile, that look that says, "I love you" It is like sharing a secret that only the two of you have.

While spontaneity is a great thing, the truth is if we wait for the perfect moment it may never come. The lives that we lead as we become busy with work, children, church, and try to exercise and eat right doesn't leave much time for spontaneity. Think of your husband/wife throughout the day as your lover, not as "daddy" or "mommy". Dream up a fantasy that you can make come true and plan to make it happen. Stop spending time dreaming of your favorite TV. Personality and telling the world how much you love to watch him/her. Stop telling your husband/wife how gorgeous your favorite super star is. No one wants to compete with the "perfect lover". None of us are perfect, but if you choose to make your spouse the love of your life you may realize you have the perfect lover for you! Genuinely compliment each other often. Share with each other your fantasy; tell each other what makes you get aroused. You might be surprised to find it is as simple as a touch as you pass by each other, a look across the dinner table, and a low voice on the telephone calling just to say "I love you".

As our children get older and more aware of what is going on in the house, you may have to be more creative or flexible with when you make love. Don't give up! When the nest is empty you can celebrate anywhere you want. Until then, you will probably be interrupted more times than you want to think about. Keeping a sense of humor will help on those evenings when you think everyone is out until 11:00, you light the candles, cook his favorite meal only to have the front door open and discover that everyone has decided to watch the game at your house. By now you have become the experts at making plan B, as you catch your lover's eye and smile; he knows exactly what you are thinking, "Breakfast may have to wait!"

When I asked another couple whom I highly respect, "How do you have a great marriage?" The woman said, "One of the keys to have a great marriage is to celebrate your anniversary every month." The husband, I believe, just smiled at her response.

Chapter 7

Now What Are You Going To Do?

In these few chapters I have said many things that can hopefully help single people and married couples in the subject of marriage. Now what are you going to do with all this information? Let me challenge you like I am challenged by every public speaker I have ever heard. I listen very attentively to the speech, and I take out of the speech what applies to me. I dissect it so that I can find practical ways to use the information. I challenge others with things that I know in my heart that must be changed immediately. After much thought, I begin walking into what I know is true for my life.

Here are some questions that you can think about:

- What was said in these pages that can possibility change the way you view marriage?
- What are the parts that you are going to hold on to and which parts are you going to throw out?
- Is experience the best teacher for marriage or is the best teacher first learning from someone else?
- How much time are you going to spend preparing for marriage?
- Do you see how a married couple could still benefit from this information?
- How important is money in your relationship?
- Are you waiting for marriage to make you whole?

One of the things that could be done now is to seek some profession counseling. Another is to seek out some type of support group for people who have had bad relationships with their parents. Or maybe some one- on-one therapy with a good psychologist could help the individual address issues that may arise in future intimate relationships. If all of this seems too much, just talking to a great friend can start to bring some healing in the area of singleness or of your marriage. In any case, get some help.

Making a decision to get married is very serious. Your choice can make you or break you. I onced heard someone say that we spend more time preparing for a driving test then we do preparing for marriage. Please do not let this be said about you. Do your homework and do not take marriage lightly.